US WOMEN'S HOCKEY TEAM

BY ANTHONY K. HEWSON

abdopublishing.com

Published by Abdo Publishing, a division of ABDO, PO Box 398166, Minneapolis, Minnesota 55439. Copyright © 2019 by Abdo Consulting Group, Inc. International copyrights reserved in all countries. No part of this book may be reproduced in any form without written permission from the publisher. SportsZone™ is a trademark and logo of Abdo Publishing.

Printed in the United States of America, North Mankato, Minnesota
042018
012018

THIS BOOK CONTAINS
RECYCLED MATERIALS

Cover Photo: Scott Mc Kiernan/Zuma Wire/Cal Sports Media/AP Images
Interior Photos: Willie J. Allen Jr./AP Images, 4-5, 24-25; Carlos Osorio/AP Images, 6-7; Gregory Shamus/Getty Images Sport/Getty Images, 8-9, 22-23; Keystone-France/Gamma-Keystone/Getty Images, 10; Jim McKnight/AP Images, 11; Bruce Bennett/Getty Images, 12-13; Mike Blake/Reuters/Newscom, 14-15; Leon Switzer/Zuma Press/Newscom, 16-17; Mark Humphrey/AP Images, 18, 20; Doug Pensinger/Getty Images Sport/Getty Images, 19; Petr David Josek/AP Images, 21; David Davies/Press Association/PA Wire URN:35151538/AP Images, 26-27; Bruce Bennett/Getty Images Sport/Getty Images, 28; Jon Gaede/Zuma Wire/Cal Sport Media/AP Images, 29

Editor: Patrick Donnelly
Series Designer: Jake Nordby

Library of Congress Control Number: 2018936264

Publisher's Cataloging-in-Publication Data

Names: Hewson, Anthony K., author.
Title: US Women's Hockey Team / by Anthony K. Hewson.
Description: Minneapolis, Minnesota : Abdo Publishing, 2019. | Series: Olympic Stars Set 2 | Includes online resources and index.
Identifiers: ISBN 9781532116087 (lib.bdg.) | ISBN 9781532157066 (ebook)
Subjects: LCSH: Hockey players--United States--Juvenile literature. | Women hockey players--Juvenile literature. | Winter Olympics--Juvenile literature. | Women medalists--Juvenile literature.
Classification: DDC 796.93092--dc23

CONTENTS

WORLD BEATERS

On home ice, just outside of Detroit, Michigan, the US national women's hockey team was poised to win another world title in 2017. Team USA had won three in a row and six of the previous seven. The United States featured some of the world's top players. Scoring star Hilary Knight skated on a line with speedy forwards Brianna Decker and Kendall Coyne. Together, they were hard to stop.

Hilary Knight (21) was one of the top scorers for Team USA in 2017.

Nicole Hensley (29) guards the net as the action heats up between the United States and Canada.

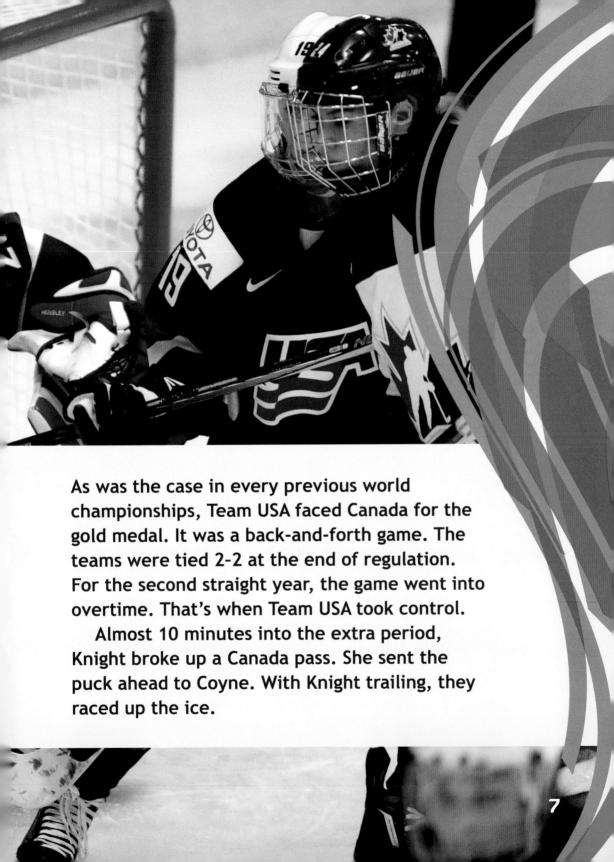

As was the case in every previous world championships, Team USA faced Canada for the gold medal. It was a back-and-forth game. The teams were tied 2-2 at the end of regulation. For the second straight year, the game went into overtime. That's when Team USA took control.

Almost 10 minutes into the extra period, Knight broke up a Canada pass. She sent the puck ahead to Coyne. With Knight trailing, they raced up the ice.

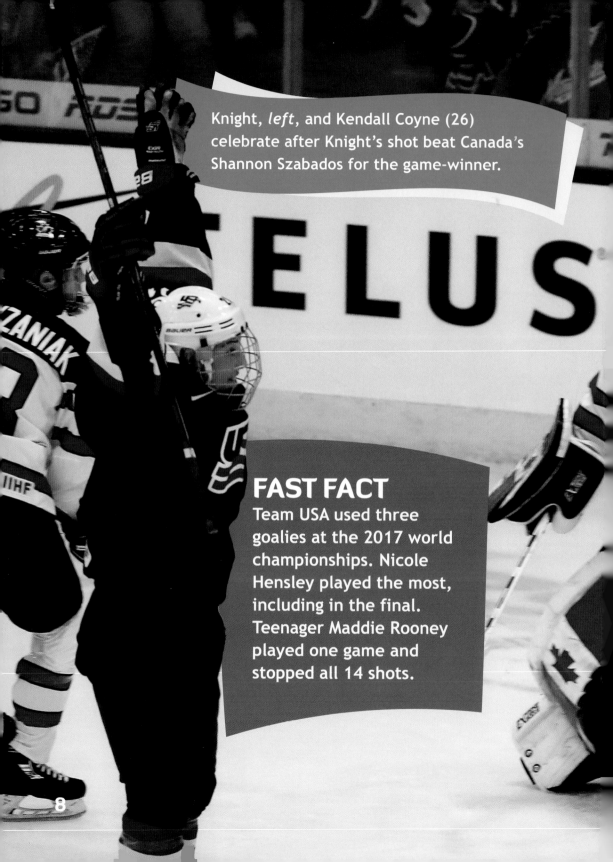

Knight, *left*, and Kendall Coyne (26) celebrate after Knight's shot beat Canada's Shannon Szabados for the game-winner.

FAST FACT

Team USA used three goalies at the 2017 world championships. Nicole Hensley played the most, including in the final. Teenager Maddie Rooney played one game and stopped all 14 shots.

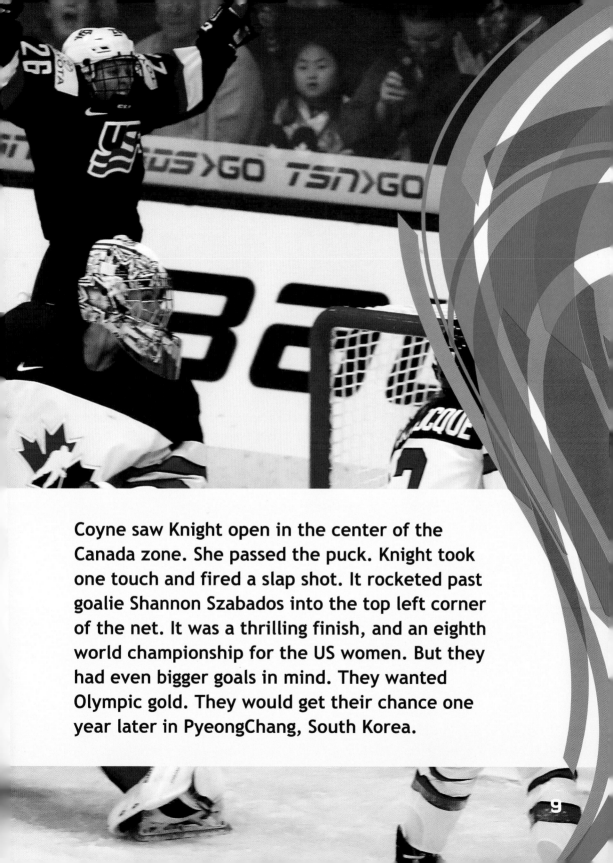

Coyne saw Knight open in the center of the Canada zone. She passed the puck. Knight took one touch and fired a slap shot. It rocketed past goalie Shannon Szabados into the top left corner of the net. It was a thrilling finish, and an eighth world championship for the US women. But they had even bigger goals in mind. They wanted Olympic gold. They would get their chance one year later in PyeongChang, South Korea.

BIRTH OF A GIANT

Hockey has been around since the late 1800s. But for most of the sport's history, girls and women had limited opportunities to participate. Most who wanted to play organized hockey had to join boys' teams. The first major international women's hockey tournament was held in 1987. At the time, the United States had just 4,000 registered female players.

That first tournament led to the first women's world championships in 1990. The US women would reach the final in the first eight times the tournament was held. But Canada denied them each time.

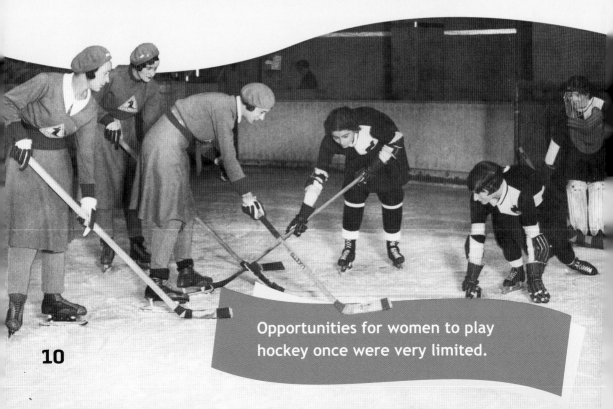

Opportunities for women to play hockey once were very limited.

Goalie Erin Whitten (34) and her US teammates line up before an exhibition game against Russia in 1997.

The United States and Canada always seemed to meet each other in big games. A fierce rivalry developed. One of the biggest games in women's hockey history came in 1998. That was the year women's hockey made its Olympic debut in Nagano, Japan. And as usual, the gold medal came down to Team USA and Canada.

Led by captain Cammi Granato, the United States had not yet lost a game at the Olympics. That continued with a 3-1 win in the final. Team USA had won the gold medal!

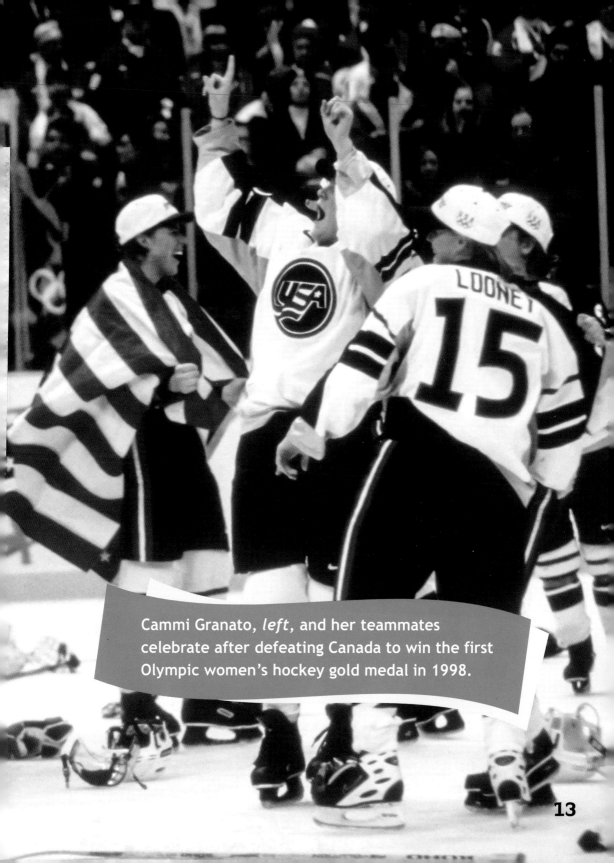

Cammi Granato, *left*, and her teammates celebrate after defeating Canada to win the first Olympic women's hockey gold medal in 1998.

Team USA suffered a painful loss to Canada on home ice in the 2002 Olympics.

FAST FACT
Through 2017, only five women had been inducted into the Hockey Hall of Fame. Two of them were Americans: Cammi Granato and Angela Ruggiero.

That game took the rivalry to a new level. And momentum shifted back and forth over the next several years. Canada beat Team USA to win the 2002 Olympic gold medal. That win came on US ice in Salt Lake City, Utah. Then Canada won the next two Olympic titles, with Team USA finishing third and then second.

The Americans had more success at the world championships. That tournament is held on non-Olympic years. Led by flashy forward Krissy Wendell and steady defenseman Angela Ruggiero, Team USA won for the first time in 2005. Going into the 2014 Olympics, the Americans had won five of the previous seven world titles. Little did they know they were about to be tested like never before.

Amanda Kessel and Team USA were playing their best hockey leading up to the 2014 Winter Olympics in Sochi, Russia.

SHOCKED IN SOCHI

Going into the 2014 Olympics, the US women felt ready. They hadn't won an Olympic gold medal since 1998. But the momentum had turned. The Americans had dominated the world championships. Now they were eager to win back Olympic gold.

Team USA had the players to do it. Forward Amanda Kessel was becoming one of the best in the world. Goalie Jessie Vetter was solid between the pipes. Now they just had to put it all together at the Olympics in Sochi, Russia.

US captain Meghan Duggan is congratulated by her teammates after scoring the first US goal against Canada in the 2014 Olympic final.

The United States and Canada met in the final again. Meghan Duggan and Alex Carpenter scored to give Team USA a 2-0 lead. The US team held on to that lead with less than four minutes to play. The players could imagine finally wearing the gold medal.

Then Canada scored. The Americans still led 2-1. Canada pulled its goalie for an extra skater. American Kelli Stack flipped a long shot at Canada's empty net, but it hit the post. Still alive, Canada tied the game with 55 seconds left. Overtime would decide it.

Marie-Philip Poulin beats US goalie Jesse Vetter (31) to tie the score in the final minute of regulation.

The US women had been so close. But Canada had caught them again. In overtime, Canada's Hayley Wickenheiser got a breakaway. Hilary Knight chased her down and hauled her to the ice. It was a penalty. On the power play, Canada scored the game-winner. Team USA had suffered another heartbreaking defeat.

That bitter feeling stayed with the players for the next four years. It inspired them to win the next three world championships. With a new coach and a new attitude, Team USA headed into the 2018 Olympics more determined than ever.

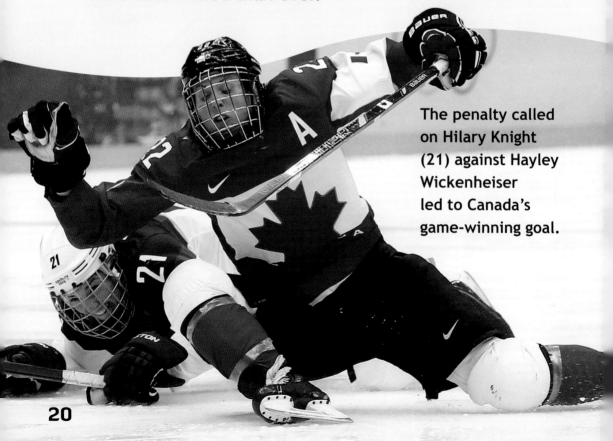

The penalty called on Hilary Knight (21) against Hayley Wickenheiser led to Canada's game-winning goal.

FAST FACT

Jenny Potter holds the US record for career points scored at the Olympic Games with 32. Potter played in four Olympic Games from 1998 to 2010.

Duggan (10), Kessel (28), and Stack console each other after their gut-wrenching loss in Sochi.

GOLDEN AGE

Robb Stauber was an assistant coach for the US team in Sochi. When he took over as head coach in May 2017, he had a plan to finally lead Team USA back to Olympic gold.

Stauber installed a new style that encouraged players to be creative. He wanted them to know they had the freedom to make their own decisions. It worked. In his first tournament as head coach, the United States won the 2017 world championships.

Robb Stauber took over behind the US bench in 2017.

FAST FACT

The US team was really serious about winning Olympic gold in 2018. The players spent much of the year before the Games living and training together in Florida.

Gigi Marvin (19) and Lee Stecklein (2) go to work in the corner against Canada at the Four Nations Cup in November 2017.

Starting in October 2017, Team USA went on a tour of exhibition games to prepare for the Olympics. Eight of the games were against Canada. The Americans started out strong, winning three of the first four. But they ended on a four-game losing streak.

The rivals met again in the opening round of play at the Olympics in PyeongChang, South Korea. Canada pulled out a close win. But the United States cruised through its other games. That set up yet another rematch: Canada vs. the United States for the gold medal.

Monique Lamoureux-Morando beats
Shannon Szabados to tie the game
in the third period in PyeongChang.

Team USA had two experienced goalies. But Stauber went with 20-year-old Maddie Rooney in the gold-medal game. The decision paid off. Rooney was rock solid in net. But Team USA trailed 2–1 in the third period.

Monique Lamoureux-Morando changed that. She picked up a pass at the blue line and fired an uncontested shot past Canada's Shannon Szabados. Once again, the Olympic gold medal had to be decided in overtime. There were plenty of US chances, but neither team could score. That meant the game would be decided by a shootout.

Jocelyne Lamoureux-Davidson, *right*, slips the puck past Szabados after making an amazing move during the gold-medal shootout.

Rooney had never played in a game this big, but she didn't show any nerves. She stopped three of Canada's first five shots. But Szabados matched her on the other end. Jocelyne Lamoureux-Davidson was next for Team USA. She skated in slowly. She faked shooting high, faked to her left, then quickly went right and buried the puck behind a sprawling Szabados.

It all came down to Rooney and Canadian star Meghan Agosta. Rooney smothered Agosta's shot, starting a huge US celebration. After 20 years, they had finally done it. Some players had been there a long time. Some like Rooney were new. But they all had the dream to become Olympic champions.

Maddie Rooney stuffs Meghan Agosta's last shot to clinch the gold medal for Team USA.

TIMELINE

1987
The US women's hockey team plays its first international game.

1990
Team USA plays in the first-ever women's world championships, losing in the final to Canada.

1998
Team USA plays in the first women's hockey Olympic tournament in Nagano, Japan, beating Canada 3-1 in the gold-medal game.

2002
The US women fail to defend their Olympic gold medal, losing to Canada on home ice in Salt Lake City, Utah.

2005
Team USA wins its first world championship, beating Canada in the final in Sweden.

2006
Team USA suffers a shocking defeat to Sweden in the Olympic semifinals and settles for bronze in Turin, Italy.

2010
Canada defeats the United States in the Olympic gold-medal game in Vancouver, British Columbia.

2014
Team USA blows a late 2-0 lead and loses to Canada in overtime in the gold-medal game at the Sochi Olympics.

2017
Team USA wins a fourth world championship in a row and its first on home ice.

2018
The US wins its first Olympic gold medal since 1998, defeating Canada in a shootout in PyeongChang, South Korea.

GLOSSARY

exhibition
A game that doesn't count in the standings.

points
In hockey, goals and assists combined.

regulation
The set time a game is scheduled to last without overtime.

rivals
Two teams or players who have an intense, ongoing competition with each other.

semifinals
The next-to-last round of a tournament.

shootout
A method of breaking a tie in which teams exchange one-on-one shots against the goaltender.

slap shot
A hockey shot in which a player takes a full backswing to strike the puck.

INDEX

About the Author

Anthony K. Hewson is a freelance writer originally from San Diego, now living in the Bay Area with his wife and their two dogs.